From the Pyramids

To the Projects

By:

Isa Born

A.K.A.

E. E. Cornell

First Printing, 2010

ISBN 978-1-257-93673-1

POLITICS

POLY = Many

TICKS = Bloodsuckers

(You draw it up).

The release of this book officially puts my life in danger. I will soon be classified as a threat for being a dangerous mind. I would like to take the time now to issue my disclaimer. I am not a terrorist, communist, racist, anarchist, or criminal in pursuit of a opportunity to commit crime. I am a lover of peace but the wool has been removed from my eyes and I will give all that I have and all that is in my power to pursue the virtue of the truth.

This is dedicated my family, Liss for your understanding, Cole for letting me spend so much time with my sons, and to the children. Seek knowledge from the cradle to the grave. Don't give up the struggle until you are free. Peace to the Universal Family including all Righteous People of the Planet Earth.

Intro:

I wonder if its ironic as the pounding in my chest slowly subsides another sleepless night is overshadowed by the stealthy steps of the Grim Reaper trying to disconnect me from the reality of existence. As the cold bony fingers tighten their grip around my heart trying for the third time this month trying to send it into fibrillation. I laugh on the inside and say to myself "back devil this heart is made out of ice," only to say it's not so easy to crush. I chuckle to myself because this time I beat him, but its like X said "Most of the time you make it, one time you wont," They call my High Blood Pressure a silent killer I call it the Grim Reaper. Funny names for a serious problem I have .I am a young man with no health insurance, not because I am lazy and shiftless man with no job or focus .On the contrary I am a very hard working young Black man ,a father, and positive role model for all my sons. When I do for one I do for all, believe me that is not easy, if you have children imagine everything you do for that child times six. I feel I could have been a positive role model for my daughter but I was not afforded with that opportunity, she is not in my life right now but I can only hope wherever she is she knows I love her. I hope she remembers the few years we had together in the beginning. But for now I can only hope that. I work as a union Building Trade Laborer Which is supposed to mean all the buildings around my county should be built by my union or my brother tradesmen. In reality it means that because I am actually certified to do the work I do, my Labor is too expensive. So I spend a lot of time on unemployment or doing side work just to survive between jobs. I don't have health insurance because it takes a certain amount of hours to be eligible and now that I have reached that amount of hours I'm going through a lot of red tape I guess they figure as long as I have been working I never really bothered them about it but about a month ago I found myself in the hospital with chest pain and my Blood Pressure was so high it registered on the Richter scale so now I have to eat a little better and shed a few pounds. I'm about 300 pounds but my woman treats me like her big teddy bear and I don't want to look like those skinny ass kids on TV. I like being a big man besides I'm not like one of those guys who looks like he's been eating donuts for so long he's become one fat lazy sack of shit. I look like that 300 pound construction worker who even though he has a beer belly you don't want to meet him in a dark alley. I took martial arts for years I did bouncer and exec protect gigs but my days of living by throwing punches, kicks and people for a living are over, I hope, I'm in my 30's now. But that to me only means my days of carefree youth are finally over. I have been blessed with some education that some people don't ever see. Some of this was instilled in me by my father ,to whom I dedicate this writing along with my son. My father is a good man and was a responsible father. I only hope to be as responsible and well respected by my son. Of course I did not always feel this way back when I knew it all (about the age of 12 maybe 13) he used to take me with him to lecture series .At a very young age I was familiarized with Dr. Ben , Ivan Van Sertima , Leonard Jefferies, Khaalid Muhammed , Malcolm X , Marcus Garvey , Louis Farrakhan, J. A. Rogers, Langston Hughes , Assata Shakur, Amiri Baraka, and a host of others too many to name . The point being at the ripe old age of about thirteen I was introduced to some history that was very different from what I was learning in World History I & II of even my elective African American studies. At this point I feel I began to transform into the man that I am. I decided at that time no matter what my profession turned out to be I would always be a professional student .It was also around that time that I became rebellious toward anything I felt was "Establishment". I was involved in political activity against my Essex County of New Jersey funded Newark Board of Education. Myself and a few other students organized a youth chapter a United Students Organization. We sat in, held rallies and marches because we had no multi-cultural curriculum. Upon graduation there were still several issues to be resolved. However I felt I had fought the good fight and simply licked my wounds and moved on. Another result of my dissatisfaction with "Establishment", magnetized me toward the streets because the people of the street were constantly involved in the struggle. The next thing that influenced my life was working for an airline which allowed me to travel somewhat abroad which satisfied some of my adventurous nature and allowed me to realize there are so many things out here beyond the street. These three things afforded me with a unique outlook and perspective. This is the foundation of my old adapted philosophy "Seek knowledge from the cradle to the grave". So now I feel it my absolute duty to share some of this perspective. This part I dedicate to my son. Though tomorrow is not promised to anyone perhaps one day he will pick up this book and see through his fathers eyes even if for a few hours. Some of the things I say may very well be seen as dangerous. Some things may be thought of as inspired. I want to take this time to say that these opinions are my own. Perhaps some of the opinions to be presented herein may be dangerous to the comfort of some. Some opinions may eventually lead to my demise. This is why I want to make a point to mention some these opinions I have not expressed to anyone and they are presented for the first time here. First let me say I am an undesirable I have made my way in and out of the criminal justice system more times than I can remember . For every crime you can imagine though I will say I have never raped a woman (even though I have been accused of it) I have always felt that rape is one of the most vicious crimes to be performed on any person male or female young or old. That being said I would also say in my opinion it is the only crime that some one cannot be reformed of because the mental disease that it roots from cannot be used in any other positive situation I can think of that being said I feel all other crimes can be reformed, and or forgiven with a few changes to the way we think of what justice is. Is the solution just if a man rapes, sodomizes, and eventually kills your 13 year old niece .Evades capture for one year is finally caught and convicted . However because evidence was improperly collected or the police did not follow procedure in effecting an arrest. The state offers him a deal of a 10 with an 18 stiff. Great he got 10 years right wrong what that means is that man will serve at least 18 months in a state prison with a protective classification which means he will have his own cell all his movements will be protected by prison officials and the only people who will surround him are people with similar situations and only during movement. So no Uncle Willie who has been in jail for five years will more than likely not even see him unless through a set of bars . So there is no family justice or payback. Is it fair? That someone who has a serious drug problem can get more time than a person like that for petty drug offences. By the way rehab is a joke in prison system drugs are more prevalent in jail than on the street. Did you ever know a person who went in clean and came home an addict? This is totally unacceptable in civilized society our criminal justice does not work on various levels. The proof positive is the high turn over rate of repeat offenders. The benefits only apply to people who invest in the now largely privatized industry of warehousing people. These are my reflections of the state of affairs of my people, country, and ancestry. PEACE.

R.I.P Lil Quan and Fredo "Big Spaz" + too many others to mention.

Chapter 1

Into Perspective
From the Pyramids

Try to relax and let's travel back approximately 5000 years and across the Atlantic Ocean nearly 10000 miles to the city of Giza. Bustling with trade, soon to be the site of perhaps back in time the world's greatest monument the great pyramid Kheops. The people look very similar to my people. Their skin is very dark tanned to a sun baked high gloss. It is in this period where we pick up our story. This was a center of great inspiration for the world and arguably most of modern technology. The construction that's taking place is that of what we know today as the First wonder of the World. The great Pyramids of Giza. This is pretty much common knowledge today, but what would not be quite as common knowledge are the facts that not only are the design unparalleled even today. There is not a structure built today that can withstand 5000 years of structural integrity. Most of modern all of modern mathematics and all of modern science is derived from this highly intelligent, highly developed society. Lots of things we consider modern have been around for thousands of years. For example it is a common belief that The Wright Brothers developed the theory of flight in the early 20th century. However 6 wooden gliders were found in tact in the pyramid at Saqqara. Present in the ancient hieroglyphics text there are images closely resembling gliders, airplanes, helicopters, a rocket, weapons of mass destruction, even what could be perceived as a micro chip and something that has been speculated as a cathode ray (television) to me it looks more like a modern light bulb. The point is if these things existed thousands of years ago why are modern people taking credit? All of the societies that are given credit with bringing great arts and sciences to the world emerged from savagery. For example the great philosophers of Greece all were either educated in Egypt. Or taught by someone who was. In ancient Greece the men who are now considered great philosophers were outcast and their ideas were largely rejected by then modern European society. To the common European man of the day was in what is generally considered to be the second Metal Age the Bronze Age (mostly developed in Northern Thailand and Southern China) before it spread through the rest of the Steppe zone of Eurasia. To him the world was flat. What we will examine is the transition of people and ideology. From great builders of Pyramids to Project dwellers, and from people who borrowed metallurgy, and casting from Mesopotamia, and the Middle East to what is considered to be the most advanced society of all time. What happened??? War for one has been a great equalizer. The libraries in Ancient Egypt have been pillaged and looted time and time again. The invaders usually kept for themselves what they could grasp, and generally burned what they could not understand or what was "unimportant". Ancient Egypt was prime real estate and many tried for their stake of the fertile "Nile Valley". Tried many times by the Hyksos, The Kyksos, The Assyrians, The Nubians, The French, The Persians, Many Arabs, and Ethiopia to name a few. All of whom achieved various levels of success and failure. Egypt has natural barriers to the east there is the Red Sea, to the west there are high cliffs. It is generally more vulnerable from the north and south. The Mediterranean Sea and the Sinai Peninsula to the north and the Nile itself provided a path from the south. In this way the culture was stolen and bootlegged across the world. Today's society is surely a byproduct of ancient society perhaps a very watered down version. We should know where we come from .That is the way to a productive future. The poorest people of the world are a sleeping giant, allowing for the most part a small fraction of people to control the destiny of the world. These people cannot control the vast populations with brute force. Instead they control the people via the media, the educational system, and by corrupt governments. These corrupt governments control by posing as spokesman of the people. They really are on a mission to control all the natural resources of the World. The general population is taught and groomed into a state of constant indifference by ignorance to the real agenda of their governments. Americans in particular have been lulled to sleep with the idea of the American Dream. Let's for a minute examine this Dream. Funny they should call it that. A big house, white pick-it fence, 2.5 children and a dog, all backed up by constitutional rights, and certain inalienable rights. Right?!? Ok sure many Americans live in a big house, with 2 or 3 kids, a dog, cable T.V., internet, a boat, a few cars, and most of the common things we buy to make life comfortable. However 90% of the things we buy are unnecessary and they only feed into us being so comfortable and satisfied with life that we don't notice what is happening to our rights, our freedoms, and our wealth (and I don't mean you credit score that is another myth. I mean real wealth, property with mineral rights that's why it's called "real estate"). All of what we as the people consider as signs of success are the baits of fools. For example the first major purchase for a lot of people I know is a new car. However as soon as you drive the car off the lot, the value decreases 30%. So if you purchase a mid-sized sedan for 20000 and entering the highway on the way to your house to show it off some idiot totals it. Your full coverage you just arranged will only pay the fair market value 14000 you will be responsible for that other 6000. Most people think that if they get a credit line for 50000 that means they have a positive 50000 to access no that means to a creditor or loan officer 50000 of debt even if you haven't spent a dime. The hard truth is that most Americans are barely above the poverty level. Think of it like this if you lost you job tomorrow, unemployment takes six to eight weeks to establish before you get one dime usually. If you are already in debt this could be the blow that makes you lose your house or apt, and you better find some thing to do with the dog, because you'll really be stuck once they come around to reposes that car (you know the one you can't hide because you just needed that GPS system because you're too lazy to read a damn map). Now how do you feed your children? What happens after they turn off the lights? The gas? The water? What happens when unemployment is further delayed or even better when it runs out and there are no extensions because all the extension money is now being funneled into the War's 2.2 billion dollar a day budget. What now? What happens when six uniformed gentlemen show up on your porch and demand that you and/or your oldest son are eligible for the draft service and must come with them immediately? What happens when they come to your home and tell you Martial is proclaimed and your legally registered Guns are now illegal, your Second Amendment rights, were negated by the Patriot Acts I &II. Here's one: "due to the establishment of Martial Law, and the fact that you have a criminal record (regardless how minor) you will report to the Work Camp XYZ for indentured servitude. Slavery was only abolished with the exception as punishment for crimes. How about due to the "Expanded Powers of police and Law Enforcement including the FBI and the new domestic roles of the CIA" we have been bugging your phone and monitoring your internet activity and you are to be placed in a concentration camp as a threat to National Security. Are you prepared for any one of these scenarios? What can we do to ensure the safety of our children and our future? How do we proceed once we wipe the remnants of hundreds of years of slumber from our eyes, and realize the people we have trusted with the protection of our rights, information, and the education of our children, are a den of thieves and murderers. We have to turn off the TV's, we have to formulate our own opinions, and protect ourselves from all enemies foreign, and more importantly domestic.

Chapter 2

The civilized enslaved by the savages

First let's examine the general concepts of slavery. By the end of
the 14th Century it became popular in Europe to take people against
their will. Definitely not a new practice or anything out of the
ordinary, slavery had already been a concept for at least a thousand
years. Generally warring factions would enslave the surviving
people of the losing army. They would be enslaved for a period
and perhaps could buy their freedom after a time of indentured
servitude they were seen still as people however a conquered
people and that does not necessarily mean they were treated well.
The rich who took slaves used the excuse that they were spreading
Christianity across the World. In the eyes of these Europeans
anyone who did not believe in Christianity was living a savage
way of life. Even though the people whom they were talking about
and supposedly modeling their life after were never Christian. To
them if you didn't believe in the Bible and follow their ways of
Christianity your life and very existence was wrong. Followers of
the Bible bear with me I do not intend to attack the Bible as
attacking ones religion or politics is the fastest way to lose ones ear
I've found, so I will tread very lightly. However the word "Bible,"
is derived from the Anglo early 14th Century root biblia and the
word simply means book. The attachment of the word "Holy," of
the Germanic heilig or the Goth hailigs which translate into "to be
preserved in tact," cast another light altogether. To say that this
book is holy is unfair in my understanding because of the amount
of translations from language to language, also because it is
understood that certain books have been omitted. These books
usually referred to as "The Dead Sea Scrolls," being left out in my
opinion negate the word holy. I think anyone who bases their life
and raises their children under a concept should fully understand it.
If you are a Christian you should read the Bible in its entirety and
know some of the history of Christians. The first widely accepted

Christian being Constantine a life-long Pagan who was baptized on his death bed in 337A.D. to unify Rome under one concept. Before that time Christians were in effect a secret society, because its concepts were considered to be heresy. There were hundreds of years between the death of Jesus Christ (A righteous Jew who taught the concepts of Freedom, Justice and Equality, and the acceptance of all people rich or poor. He also taught the leaders of the so called Churches were not to be trusted every man is his own Church, and said to the Pharisees in the Psalms "Surely you are all Gods Sons of the most high.") And the wide acceptance of Christianity. This is one of the concepts taught to slaves to keep them slaves. Along with separation concepts spoken of on the bank of the James River in 1712 by Willie Lynch (Who spoke of breaking of slaves mentally more so than physically). The concept of separation is what still controls the masses to this very day. It's been said "the greatest trick the devil ever pulled is to convince the world that he does not exist." Well the main reason most people do not come together and do something about the atrocities of Government, is because they do not identify with their neighbor. Too busy saying he isn't like me he's from Jamaica , or Puerto Rico, or Haiti, or London, or some where in Africa, or he's one of those Muslims, or he is Christian, or he's white, or a host of other reasons. Old people do not identify with the young. So how do we as young people benefit from the experience of our elders? Women do not identify with the men so how we have a functional family? These are the effects of a new kind of slavery that was developed during the American slave trade. The effects of which still effect every level of society to this day. The people that were subjected to this slave trade system were part of some of the worst atrocities in all of history not because they were beaten and degraded, because they were separated from their identity. Let me give an example of what I mean and you judge for yourself. A ship docks off the western coast of the African Continent 20 men exit 7 of what we call crewmen, 7 Africans who have been working with them as guides and / or helping with language barriers and 6 lets call them traders or as I call them scouts. They came into the village with help of guides enter under the guise of trade and missionary duties. They developed a relationship with the people. Soon they became a watchful eye as to when the strike should be made. The hunting party goes out to search for food or whatever and are ambushed and trapped by the people laying in wait. They are shackled and dumped into the hold of the waiting ship. Like those poor crabs on the "Deadliest Catch," program, Literally stacked on top of each other until the ship hold is at its capacity. There is no bathroom, and please don't be claustrophobic or have a weak stomach because the smell of human feces, urine and vomit prevail many people die because the methane gas produced naturally by a few hundred people displaces oxygen. The people have been purposely placed away from people of their tribe, or even those who spoke their language. One family some how stays in close proximity a pregnant mother, father, a son and one daughter. After weeks of the torturous voyage the ship dock again in one of the Caribbean Isles and the holds are emptied the family above is gathered together. The mother is separated from the father kicking and screaming. Adding to the fathers already broken down sense of manhood, and in front of the entire family the unborn child is cut from her womb. Then the man is separated from the already traumatized children, and in front of them is castrated. Thus teaching the children by fear who has the power. Next English, Spanish, Portuguese, or French is established as the only language to be used by the young now broken pair, now mentally branded to be obedient slaves. After reaching the final destination of the voyage the separations are further implicated. The young children are not given shoes or pants yet they do not have to work. The older slaves who have to work resent the children and think they have it easy. The children resent the elders because they have shoes and pants. The women lose faith in the men because the men can't protect her from rape, forcible sodomy, or other atrocities by Massa Jones, his Overseer, or His Sons. So she in turn teaches her daughter not to trust the black man because he can't help her out of bad situations. Also teaching the sons that they won't amount to any thing. Which causes dissent in both directions and between the siblings? Then Massa takes his slave born children from the field and places them in his home and tells them their darker brothers and sister is not to be trusted and to watch them. Creating an extra level of security, with everybody hating each other. Who has time to hate Massa Jones? He is loved and seen as the only friend by many slaves regardless of beating and other cruel acts. These concepts are taught to the children and passed down from generation to generation from that time to this it is not uncommon to hear "Niggas can't get together on nothing," or "You can't trust a Nigga". I in my life time have heard older aunts one in particular say I had good hair as opposed to nappy hair. If these concepts are still alive the self hate they beget still exists. This is the reason along with the fact that the images we look up to (usually on TV) live beyond what we can afford. Many of us turn to crime and the streets. It is the only way many people see to get ahead. This is known which is why more than 90% of young Black urban males from my community wind up in some phase of the criminal justice system by the time they are 25. Why is that? Why is it that youth identify with gangs more than family? For the same reasons it was true in 1712. It's not true that we don't make any progress in society. Nearly every major invention of modern time came from People of African decent. However I don't really know if the gentleman who invented the automatic transmission or the gentleman who invented the cotton gin or even more popular figures like Louis Latterman who invented the filament for the modern light bulb without which Thomas Edison's light bulb surely would not have been such a hit. Did any of them receive patent rights? Inventions like the stoplight would surely fuel some of the richest most powerful men in the world being on every street corner and all. Every time our people begin to realize these facts and organize on any level they are imploded from within. By groups like Co-Intellpro. Who destructed movements like the Black Panther Party and Black liberation Army from within and without. The drugs that followed only completed the process of lulling people back to sleep. The generation gap is perpetuated because in the sixties there was a Black Power Movement. Somehow and for some reason that scared the powers that be in government. So the old cartoon concept was brought into play "if you can't beat em join em," So there were parties and the new drug of a generation was introduced Cocaine. I don't care what group of people deny it everybody got in on the movement from the music industry to the fashion industry . Black people were told to come and party among the Whites for the first time some of them had been wishing for that the whole time. The brothers who complained about unfair work practices got jobs. They were told to calm down this a time for "Free love," and "Peace," and all the bad people are behind the war in Vietnam, "but trust me I'm your friend. Cocaine is a party drug everybody is doing it you cant even get hooked on it, if you put it on your dick it'll stay hard", lots of people fell for that BS and these same people who fought so hard to go to school, and become doctors, and Principals and secretaries, were now hooked on cocaine as a weekend drug and when they were told you get high faster when you freebase it they jumped at the chance. Giving way to the Crack Epidemic. My generation is the next generation to follow and many of us couldn't look up to our mothers, fathers, aunties, and uncles on crack. There was no such thing as a crack head until 1980. Now uncle who had a degree from an Ivy League School is running around selling cans to chase the crack. We as young men even call the people we see getting high "Auntie," or "Unc". All the Black Power Knowledge is effectively cut off from the younger generation. We as youth can't look up to our elders who actually got an education and actually went thru a struggle because they were taken purposely out of that mindset. So we tell ourselves we've gotta pull ourselves up by our bootstraps and grind or hustle. Nothing is wrong with that every group of people that were naturalized into this country were criminals first. Eventually they organized and sank the monies into legitimate industry and went straight. We don't have a home country we identify with so we give it all to the lottery the preacher man whose dreams are getting more and more expensive. Not all the youth of my generation fell for the hype though. It is obvious through the progression of the music. In the late 80's it must have scared someone else because once again through the music the next drug of choice was introduced to my generation. Weed you know the "Gateway Drug," nobody really ever worried about. I remember every other song was about a forty and a blunt. It was just a party drug sounded a little like something I had heard before but when they came with "it comes from the Earth so," it's natural I said to myself what about every other poison aren't they natural too? All the "Fight the power," songs faded to the back and off the radio air play lists. They were replaced by what I like to call the lets get high and forget, or don't worry be happy type songs. Weed I remember used to be something people smoked and laughed joked but only wound with the munchies. Now the weed that people smoke has an entirely different effect. People can't even wake up and eat unless thy smoke they don't feel right. That kind of reminds me of the effects of Opiates. Wherein people feel sick in the morning until they get a morning fix. This generation has largely been once again lulled to sleep. As major changes take place in the world. September 12, 1991, George Bush announced the beginning of the New World Order out of these troubled times. Our people slumber as this unfolds and the few rights and freedoms they believe they have, fade into memory. We the American People have been place into chains. The statement New World Order means one world Government. Our Government leaders have conspired under our noses to not only sell us out but are committed to World domination. In the beginning of this chapter we examined the basic ideology of slavery. We as American people outside the very exclusive club of super rich Controlling Elite, have been led back into a Physiological Slavery. Which may very well lead to some form of physical bondage whether that means labor camps, concentration camps or The Dreaded Draft? There is glaring evidence that our children are subjected to an inferior education process which generally only prepares them for some form of manual labor, a military career, or some meaningless mid- level business career. I'm not trying to take away from what people do to feed their families I perform manual labor and it pays the bills when work is available however I will never ever work my way into a position of Super Rich Controlling Elite, by working for anybody. I don't remember any classes that taught me to start my own business, invest my money, or even raise my children for that matter.

Chapter 3

Secret Ties

Many member of our Government, local, state, and federal, have subversive ties to secret organizations. Many people have heard of Masons, Elks, Shriners, Knights of Columbus, Knights of Malta, Skull and Bones, Scroll and Key and countless other organizations in our society. They are seen but not seen, and are generally thought of as harmless Good Old Boy clubs that can get you out of a traffic ticket with a high sign or secret handshake if the judge is member. However it is not common knowledge that these organizations count in their membership most of our elected officials, most of our law enforcement, and most of the religious leaders in our society. This would all be fine if these people had our best interest at heart. This is not however the case. The goal of a secret society generally remains hidden that is the function of the secrecy. The lower members are not even privy to the real goals of the societies. They are simply baited in with the promise of always having the Brotherhood to fall back on in times of legal or financial hardship, that the mysteries of the Universe will be revealed to them, and that they will eventually be among the enlightened ones. Some don't realize that the rituals they take part in, and are not allowed to talk about are actually rituals that worship Satan. High ranking Scottish Rite Masons of the 31 degree and beyond can never utter the name of their true God "Jah Bul Lon," never to be spoken in public by any Mason. This is not the same "God worshipped by Christians even though most ministers I have met are Masons. The meaning of this word translates as across between the Jewish " Jehovah", the Pagan "Baal" which is Infinite God head of Satan, and "Osiris" who was the Egyptian God of the Dead. According to Albert Pike late 19th Century 33rd degree Mason, this is the God to be spoken of and worshipped by Scottish Rites Masons of the 30th, 31st, and 32nd degrees. Only high ranking Masons or one's with Illuminated degrees are privy to this knowledge. All lesser members are simply cattle. The Illuminated ones or members of the Illuminati are conspiring world domination. They believe that since they are the only ones who realize what is going on in the world they are Elite. They use media, and propaganda outlets to perform mass mind control on the general population. The Television's cathode ray is a mass hypnosis experiment in the full stride of success. The subliminal messages flashed across the screen causes the consumers to buy for example, Jordach Jeans or Grower's Pride orange Juice. It can also influence young people into military service. When the issues being fought over are not in the interest of the people, or even moral high grounds. The issues of war are always based on financial gain. Not always as obvious as our Strong Arm President I like to call "Jed Clampet," having an Oil Empire, or even invading the country with the largest supply of Poppies for Opium production. Every place in the world where there is civil unrest and there is a major money making natural resource, the influences of these societies are present. Why do you think that in South America, Central America, China, North Korea, formally Iraq, and all over Africa horrible atrocities take place and "Rebels" attack for seemingly no reason killing women and children? This is part of the plan. WAR IS BIG BUSINESS. It does not matter whether it is on the side right or wrong. What matters is that IT IS CONTINUOUS. Which is why the myth of The Cold War was propagated so long? The people who make the weapons are the same one who run countries and own Haliburton, entire oil Conglomerates, also own Springfield Arms and other weapon producing companies. The same families who financed Hitler's Third Reich including and especially the George Bush's family. Those who not only did illegal wartime trading with a wartime enemy (Germany) they also provided weapons, pig iron, a large percentage of wartime steel, and ammunition to the enemy. Prescott Bush our President's grandfather was caught and was supposed to be tried for treason but like Grandfather like Grandson that never came to pass. War works well on another level for the so called Elite. They believe in "Population Control." So why not send your children off to die in some God forsaken land 12000 miles away, their children will never go. So the population get into check., The propaganda is spread, more weapons are sold, all while stealing or exploiting whatever resource we invaded for. Whether that be Oil, Diamonds, Cocaine, Opiates, gold or whatever. It's the same thing if we send the CIA to train rebels to fight against a government for any of the above. Where do you think every group of terrorist, rebels or any other kind of anti-government fighters get weapons, training, or other skills of basic anarchy? Why do you think they kill women and children? In a speech to Congress in the mid fifties George Bush then a Senator gave a speech on the sterilizations of "Lesser Peoples." It wasn't outrageous during that time for a government official to refer to Black or Hispanic people in that fashion. Several years later when he got into the vice presidency on Reagan's ticket. He obviously saw his opportunity to seize power and Reagan was shot 30 days after his inauguration. Maybe there is no connection but right around that time his other son Neil was seen having lunch with the brother of John Hinckley Jr. the man who shot Reagan. The Pope whom was also shot within those power seizing first few months. The then Pope John Paul II was an ex-poison gas sales man during World War II who fearing punishments for war crimes changed his name and joined the church, also had his own ideas about who should be in power. The secret ties of George Bush landed him in full power after March 30, 1981. They did not even have to deny the facts surrounding the attempted Coup D'ETAT. In fact they confirmed most of them. The so called Illuminated ones are at the head of all major financial organizations, all heads of state answer to these Higher Powers. The people who are part of these organizations are not loyal to any one Government they believe in one World Government so any Presidential Oaths or such taken are fully overshadowed by loyalties to these Secret Societies. These men do not fear the people who put them in office the only power they have is to take that position away. They are much more concerned with the men and women who move behind the scenes in the shadows. They have the power to take away much more than a position. All Secret Societies put their members under a penalty of death. They cannot reveal the inner workings of the society or any secret pertaining to the organization. Some even have to deny membership. Especially members of The Order of the Druids, The Order of the Golden Dawn, The Skull &Bones, The Scroll &Key, The Priory Of Scion, The Bilderburg Group, Council on Foreign Relations, and lots of others. Most of these organizations have a totally different agenda from the ones propagated by the Public Officials they count among their members. The real evil behind these power hording organizations is that they all know the true secret of life. Though it has been hidden from the public for thousands of years, it is beautiful in it's simplicity. The mind is the greatest resource a man has because through positive thought reality can manifest. This is why so many distractions are pumped into the minds of the public, so they can continuously be used as a tool, and or a slave, never use their mind to its full potential, and remain complacent with their lives as they are. This is the true meaning of enlightened ones or "Illuminati," they hold this secret to themselves so that the common man cannot experience nor benefit from the power of his own great mind. Thought power is magnetic so if you think small you get small, if you believe small your existence will not matter, however if you think great and begin to realize your potential no one can stop you. On the other hand as long as you believe your only rewards will come in "Heaven," you concentrate only on what happens after death and perhaps your life goes to waste. So realize all the great powers of the Universe you have the potential to tap into as long as you stop wasting your time wasting away. This is a reality that many have killed for and many more have died for.

Chapter 4

Disappearing Law

There are many rights and much Constitutional law that has been
either undermined or basically amended out of context. Does
anybody remember Laws of the Land were governed by and
compared and contrasted to The Constitution of The United States?
There was an entire Branch of Government dedicated to
interpreting these Laws, The Judicial Branch right? Well as many
Americans have slept the last 10 years away. Lots of shady
business has transpired. A couple presidencies have been stolen in
full view of the public. Thousands of people were murdered on
September 11, 2001 (10 years to the date after the first Bush
President made his New World Order speech). Terrorist were
blamed, however every Major Media Organization in the world
outside the U.S. reported an Insider Trading Scandal in connection
with the September 11th Attacks. Stock Options were purchased
that basically made it obvious of the involvement of the purchaser.
. The London Times called it the Largest Insider Trading Scandal
in the history of the World. Somebody via a dummy Company
invested billions on insurance options in the event the Building
collapsed. Coincidence perhaps, but I've learned coincidence is
usually coincidental for a reason. I watched a movie "The long kiss
goodnight," 2 weeks before with the same scenario. The
Government Agency needed funding for whatever so they were
going to kill 3000 Americans via bomb. They had the scapegoat all
lined up too (they had an Arabian National frozen to be crashed
into a ditch so Terrorist would be blamed). I remember Sept. 11,
2001, I lost friends and I watched the drama unfold I smelled a rat
from the very beginning. I have been watching buildings come
down for years my business is demolition. I am not afraid to admit
in my professional opinion the buildings were professionally
imploded. Don't take my opinion for it visit the site. Then visit the
site of any professionally imploded project. The Pentagon Building

was never hit by an aircraft. Don't take my word for it visit the Web Site Hunt the boeing.com. These were the first pictures taken by Army Intelligence you can't get more official than that. The first pictures taken of the Pentagon while Emergency Vehicles were still present did not contain any aircraft wreckage. Thirty Two hours after the dust settled they were already blaming Bin Laden. A CIA operative funded by US Taxpayer dollars. Al Quida funded, trained, and armed by the US. Sadaam Hussein was never a problem until he invaded Kuwait an Oil Producing country. Who still practice human slavery to this day? The murder of Sadaam's Sons on the front page of every paper was an outrage. I say all this to point out that there has been no UN Tribunal to investigate the War Crimes of the Bush Administration. The torturing of countless Arab Nationals and Muslims interned at the beginning of the conflict and locked away ever since. All these things legal according to the Patriot Acts I & II .Which states: The definition of terrorism is broadened. Foreign Government now have the right to expedite in the US., State and Local governments have expanded powers to spy on citizens, religious organizations, political organizations, with no probable cause. Arrest of "terror suspects", with no probable cause. FBI expanded powers to obtain personal info, arrest without probable cause, a Field Supervisor can write a National Security Letter that can allow searches or sneak peeks with no Judge's OK. Pressure Media to reveal sources with threat of fines and imprisonment. Mere suspicion can have you detained for a period of up to six months without a review. The detained Arab nationals and Muslim Political Prisoners is not Public Record. There are also new restrictions of access to haz-mat information. They now have the power to deport immigrants and give them no power to challenge via Habus Corpus. Full power is vested in the President to write Law and declare War. The strange and expanded Powers of law enforcement agencies are nothing compared to the powers vested in the new Homeland Security group of law enforcement officials. The Homeland Security along with the powers of FEMA is the farthest reaching law enforcement agency to date. Once Martial Law is established FEMA in effect will run the country having been granted these powers by the President. In these documents a parallel government is being prepared and trained to run the country in the event of total FEMA control. We will not elect them they will simply control perhaps behind the scenes like now, possibly in the forefront. They are the most dangerous to those of us who would like to believe in the guarantees of the Constitution and it's Amendments. WE THE PEOPLE are in for some very tough times ahead if we don't hold our public officials accountable while we still have the power.

Chapter 5

Criminal Justice System

The criminal justice system of the US is another highly flawed
system. The only real accomplishment of this system is the
warehousing of poor people into a system of legal slave labor. In
Newark N.J. we live in a Police State right now. The police ride in
convoys with their light constantly on. They enforce the policies of
central Government, rather than responding primarily to criminal
misdeeds. They spy on and intimidate normal citizens to plant fear
rather than investigate and catch criminals. The powers that be still
in line with the "Willie Lynch" doctrine promote separation of the
family. Approximately 87% of urban Black males have entered
some phase of the criminal justice process by the time they are 25
years old. This is because there is no real recreation in the inner
city readily available. There is plenty of money allocated for youth
centers and such but it either is not enough or it is being
misappropriated. As they grow up in the midst of recycled high
crime areas, they are subjected to law enforcement officials that
are not concerned with the betterment of the community. They are
more concerned with quotas. This is why there are hundreds of
arrests daily for "Loitering or Wandering in a drug area". I don't
know where the lawmakers grew up but everywhere in my
neighborhood is a drug area. Nobody in my neighborhood has the
ability to transport CDS into our neighborhood. However much
like the Pharmaceutical Industry the Justice System is more
interested in treating of symptoms than finding a cure. How is it
that a man can be sent to prison for years for selling a product that
is imported mainly by Government officials? The people who are
made into examples are the very bottom of the Totem Pole. This
begins to illustrate a very obvious Double Standard. Money is the
only thing that can buy Justice. When you are from a poor area it is
more like JUST US or maybe it's JUST- ICE. The only way to
have a chance is to have money. We have always been Guilty until

Proven Innocent. We are arrested and detained without any hearing and held for periods of up to 10 months. The system will constantly dangle freedom in front of us in return for a conviction. Whether that means accepting the false sense of security provided by BS programs like P.T.I. or Probation, I don't care what they call it. IT WILL COUNT AS A CONVICTION ON YOUR PERMANENT RECORD. Drug offenses disqualify many opportunities for employment, and IF CONVICTED OF A DRUG OFFENSE YOU WILL NOT QUALIFY FOR PELL GRANTS AND CERTAIN OTHER STUDENT LOANS. This also serves to separate the families. A man is convicted, and his family is left to fend for themselves. The woman may be forced to apply for government assistance. The next phase of separation is set into play by uplifting the woman. The Government provides housing, food, and perhaps an education to the single woman in return for placing the man on Child Support. This insures when he returns home he will already be in debt and on his way back. for Non-Support. This makes the woman resent the man because she feels she does not need him the Good Government will provide for her. It is my opinion that every crime with the exceptions of rapes and child molestation has the potential to be a career path for some one if the focus wasn't so much on Slave Labor provided by the Prison Population. The Prisons and jails are major money making industries. They provide free slave labor for various industries. They spend 99 cents per day on each prisoner's meals. They also work it into the system that people spend at least 8 days in the system even for petty crimes. After this period has elapsed they are provided with a grant for each prisoner. (Apprx. 10000) These poor people get into the system and are generally given the highest bail possible in relation to the offense. This in my opinion is not the benefit of the doubt or Innocent until proven guilty, its conviction until you can come up with bail, there is no legal representation, no law books to study or any review. Those are all things of the past. If you are arrested and you have no family to make moves for you on the outside you can sit about 10 months or

180 working days before they have to indict you. Many people cop out under the pressure of having to sit that long before even being heard for review or trial. This is how many weak cases come to count as convictions for the State. If a man ha s been sitting in jail for six months and the Judge tells him if he pleads guilty he'll get probation and go home, or he can go back and wait on a trial date, many men would take going home. I personally have been arrested more than twenty times for various reasons. I am not gonna sit here and tell you I was always innocent of every thing but most of the time I got arrested I was not guilty. I have 2 felony convictions and they both fall under the above example I just didn't want to sit and eventually got an offer I didn't refuse. I have only been read Miranda Rights once in my life. I have spent 8 days in jail for Wandering in Drug Area on a block I happened to live on. Only to have the case dismissed. I have been brutalized, robbed, by Black Racist Police who hate themselves. They generally have a Napoleonic Complex because somebody took their lunch money in high school and chased them home everyday. Back on track the point is the system is geared to destroy the Black Family. There is no real rehabilitation in place. If you don't provide real role models the only role models we have to latch on to are on TV. All of them live beyond our means. Why not rehabilitate car thieves by teaching them to be Repo-Men. Rehabilitate Home Invaders, Murderers, or Kidnappers by sending them for military training, or Mercenaries. Grifters, Drug Dealers, and Scam Artists can work for the CIA. Gang Members can be the Police or National Guard. Racketeers or Loan sharks can work for the IRS. Those guilty of Theft by Deception can be Politicians. I think Rape and Molestation is Mental Disease therefore I offer no solution. However consider the above solutions seriously most of them are already in place but only apply to the Privileged. Those that can buy their way out of a conviction or into most any thing else. A life of privilege can buy freedom or a less harsh sentence. Any system of Justice that succumbs to bribery is fundamentally flawed. Any groups of people that accept this kind of Justice and

practice this system of law are inherently evil, and are only concerned with greed. I know I speak only for myself when I say "I WILL DO WHATEVER IS NECESSARY TO FEED MY CHILDREN REGUARDLESS OF WHOM OR WHAT. NO LAW OF THE LAND WILL DISUEDE ME FROM PROVIDING FOOD, CLOTHING, AND SHELTER FOR MY BABIES. ANYTHING THAT NEEDS TO BE DONE WILL BE WITHOUT HESITATION OR CONSIDERATION OF THE UNFAIR LAWS OF THE LAND. I DO NOT CONSIDER ANY LAW OF THE LAW OF THIS TAINTED LAND APPLICABLE. DO NOT STAND IN MY WAY, I WILL GO OVER AROUND OR THROUGH YOU IF NECESSARY. ANY MAN INTERFERING WITH THE FEEDING OF THE BABIES HEAD SHALL BE TAKEN OFF BY THE SWORD. THAT IS NOT A FIGURE OF SPEECH I AM PREPARED TO DIE OR KILL TO FEED MY BABIES. ". I agree with Ernesto " Che" Guevara " We cannot be sure of having some thing to live for unless we are willing to die for it." I am prepared to sacrifice for my children. Any man who would not is a coward and is already dead in the eyes of the World. The prison system in closing is a maximum profit minimum expenditure system. From a business stand point it would certainly be a wise investment if there weren't human lives at stake. The rehabilitation process is a joke or a reoccurring trap depending on how you look at it. It really needs to be rethought. A real system of rehabilitation should be considered with real programs. This current system has not worked it is time for a Plan B.

Chapter 6

Non-Threats

Obviously there are exceptions to the rule of undereducated Urbanites remaining on the bottom of the Totem Pole. Lots of very seemingly successful people come from an urban background. This makes it seem like the other people who are not quite as successful are doing something wrong. This is not necessarily the truth. Some people are allowed to become what we commonly call tokens. These individuals pose no threat to the plans of the powers that be and are generally used as an example of success stories. Most of these people are women. The Government is more likely to set up programs for urban females. This further separates her from her man who very well may be in some phase of the Correctional System. This further breaks down the family structure. This is why a woman is more eligible for Welfare, Housing, or School benefits if she is single. A woman is considered to be less of a threat to the Establishment. This is why a Black Woman is more likely to be moved up the Corporate Ladder. It tackles a Double Minority when Companies are reviewed by Affirmative Action. Women are also less likely to Make Waves in a male dominated environment. Gay Men are also a likely choice they are so happy that they are being accepted. They may talk smack but they won't make waves. A lot of the people in Power Positions are into lots of weird, and/or gay activities in their private lives. If a lot of these activities became public it could cause embarrassment to Public Image. So the Gays are kept happy to keep quiet and/ or for future reference. They are not viewed as a threat because they are not fully accepted by society. Generally the only community influenced by the activity of a gay man is the Gay Community. The real power of "The Powers That Be, is separation in the Community. Everybody is yelling Black Power, White Power, Gay Pride, Woman Power, Puerto Rican Pride..ECT but we all lose power by way of separation. If we can learn to stop putting up our own barriers by saying things like: I'm not like those Christians, Muslims, Five Per centers, Black Guys, White Guys, Niggers, Spics, Fags, Jabookies, Goombas, Dikes, Yankees, Chinks, Gooks, Towel Heads, Camel Jockeys, Dot Heads, Nerds, Geeks, Jocks, Weirdoes, Rednecks, Jews, Nazis, Democrats, or any other derogatory term used to downgrade people. We need to think about how we can come together and stand up for our rights. The individuals who are given a pass have to see their way back to the trenches. We are all in this together. We all have a problem called "New World Order." It means a reorganization of the Class system. There will only be two Classes under New World Order Super Rich and very poor. The Super Rich is to be a World controlling Class of Elite. The very poor are to be a Class of slaves of a Mental Death. The numbers of the poor people are being reduced in astronomical proportions. We have to get out of the mind set of automatons. If you find yourself in the position of a non threat that does not mean you are exempt from the rule. It means you are in a position of strength and should feel obligated to work toward the common cause. We can no longer let the separations of race, class, creed, religion, culture, sexual orientation, or position in life come between The People. If we don't stand together we will fall for anything. Wake up from the matrix of lies and vast webs of deceit. Everything is not O.K." We The People," are being lied to. Good Government has become a nest of snakes. Ready to strike at any of "We The People," that stands in their way in their great quest for The World's Resources.

Chapter 7

All Powerful

"We the People," posses the power to change the direction of the World. We as Americans have the strength to truly be a world power. All the people of World come to America because it is the "Land of Opportunity". We have a truly diverse society. We are the largest gathering of consumers on the Planet. The amount of food we throw away can feed half the starving people of the World. The technology we take for granted and / or retard the development of can solve all the fossil fuel problems of the World. The minds we lock away can be some of the greatest artists, poets, singers, writers, dancers, fighters, and / or leaders in the World today. The money we spend on cable television, designer clothing, and jewelry can put millions of poor deserving children through college. We have the votes, the numbers and if necessary the guns to retake our government. We just have to put both hands back on the wheel, and turn off the autopilot. It's not enough to go to work 40-60 hours a week, get paid, pay the bills, buy you drug of choice, have sex with the partner of your choice, eat sleep, shit, and settle down in front of the television until its time to go back to work.. You have to make the first step. We need some medium that does not separate us by Religion, Culture, Sexual Orientation, Political Party, Race, Sex, or any thing else that will separate us as people. Black people we are the largest group of consumers in support of people other than ourselves. We buy every Timberland boot, Nike sneaker, Red Monkey Jean, and Diamond encrusted jewel. What we could do with just one year of that spending power. We are taxed without any semblance of representation. We need Black Conglomerates. This is the way that we as a people can make it in today's World. Don't get it twisted every group of people that was naturalized into this country had a criminal element. The Italians had La Cosa Nostra, The Polish, The British, The Jews, The Triads, The Yakuza, The Mexican Mafia, The Jamaican Posse and on and on. There is a glaring difference between these people and American Black Men. They all have somewhere they can identify with as home away from here. They can send money back and leave if it gets too hot, before they go legit. Eventually needs to out grow criminality and go "Legit," that's where the real money is. Controlling an industry for example if we controlled the sanitation industry (Italians), had a hold on banking industries (Jews), or even a few big Oil Industries Bushes), then we would be able to leave our children more than money, we could leave real wealth and a legacy, instead of an estate. My point is the power exists within the conscious consumer. For all the power and influence possessed by big government what they lack is man power. The real foot soldiers of the mighty Elite are people like you and me. The Police, National Guardsmen, Army, Navy Air Force, Marines, and any Government Agency you can think of usually does not consist or any real Power Mongers. We the Little people need to realize we are a Sleeping Giant. A group of minds, most of which are in a dormant stage. It seems to me to be a running joke that a "Mind is terrible thing to waste", However in my experience I have noticed many minds intentionally lay to waste. It is also quoted that most humans only use only 7-10% of their brain capacity. Is that not a dreadful waste? We who are many posses real power to influence the few. However most of us do the opposite. The first step in regaining our control is to learn to control ourselves. Joe Q. Public needs to take a long hard look in the mirror. He needs to realize that if we don't put our differences aside we are all headed for self destruction by default. Some feel these are insurmountable goals but we will never know if we don't try. We need to look past all our differences and realize the glaring similarities. No one I know lives completely within their means. There is the myth of credit in reality this is called debt. I will present an example. If you qualify for a 100000 credit card this means an extra 100000 right? Wrong! What this means is you have a highly liquid asset that can be accessed at any time. Which when it comes to being approved for a loan is considered and actually can count against you. The value of the dollar is no longer counted against the Gold Standard. The dollar is on a system of borrowing against itself and X amount of dollars are printed for every 1 dollar of Gold standard value. That's why prices go up every year. The government is spending all the vast acquired wealth of the past 330 years. All the funds amassed by the free labor of slavery. The Sweat Shop style cheap labor that fueled the industries of the north. When it was discovered that it was cheaper to simply pay a laborer a penance than to feed and cloth his entire family. All the land stolen from American Original People (commonly referred to as "American Indians", which only further cements the idea of how lost Columbus really was.) All the criminals, rapist, and undesirables released form European Prisons to become Colonist and Founding Fathers. All the Oil is even now being stolen by President Jed Clampet and his crew but we still are being forced to pay 3$ a gallon at the pump. Sounds like Enron plenty of power so lets shut down a few generators to make a high demand and hundreds of millions of dollars. Big Oil has plenty of stolen free oil so why not shut down a few refineries to make a high demand. The only solution to this is for the people take a stand together. Granted many of us including myself have become very dependent on fossil fuels. Nevertheless we can still give them hell at the pump if we as Americans boycott Exxon, Mobil, BP, and Texaco, for the next five years and only use Mom and Pop businesses for fuel gas will be about 50 cents a gallon by the time we finish. WE can also all pay at the pump with pennies in protest. No fancy wrapped coins from the bank just those old sticky pennies from between the seat cushions. Hell they want to squeeze extra pennies out of us lets give them to them. It is legal US tender and if you say "fill it up", they'll be forced to take them especially if that's all you have on you that day. Can you imagine the slow down that would cause if the next 1000 people that pulled into Exxon paid with a sack of green sticky pennies? Can you imagine the slow down at the banks? Some body in power would feel it soon enough. Besides 17 year old Billy Bob quitting his summer job in hurry, who would it hurt? Not you, your life wouldn't skip a beat providing you allow a little extra travel time. Now imagine you paid all the pesky bill collectors with pennies. There is a quiet revolt for you. The next time some teenager calls you about some delinquent bill ask if they take cash and tell them you'll be there directly. Stop by your bank first change that 300$ they have been bothering you about into a 200 pound sack. Give them the pain in the ass for a change. This is a simple way for you personally to rebel. Do it once just to see the look on someone's face or to shut up that pesky bill collector for a few months. If something like this done on a large scale things can really get shaken up. This is a simple and maybe far fetched example but this is how we need to think. Instead of saying "I can do nothing," we need to say "What can I do?" or "What difference can I make and how?" After we have exhausted our words, our time, our fists, and if necessary our bullets we still need to be using our mind to guide the direction of our struggle. The mind is the most powerful tool we have and we have to use it against those who oppose our well being. Be they Government Officials, Law Enforcement Officials, or Joe Blow the neighbor.

Chapter 8

Teach the children

No matter what you believe in one thing is certain one day your
physical body will return to the essence from whence it came.
Those of us who have children have a responsibility to them. I was
into the street life for a long time. Lots of things are a matter of
public record. Other things will remain among unsolved mysteries.
One day I realized that my children have to rely on me for not only
food, clothing, and shelter but for some kind of legacy. I have
made many mistakes and if my children don't know my history
they may very well be doomed to repeat it. So now I make it my
business to spend as much quality time and energy on my children
as I can. Those of my children that I have access to. Confidently
one day I will be able to build a relationship with my oldest child.
Regrettably right now that is not the case. I teach my boys some of
the pitfalls of life that I have personally encountered. I know that I
need to share all my vast experience with them good and bad. That
way they can take from that what they can use. I also realize I need
to prepare them to carry on as men on their own. "The children are
the future", is an understatement. The Father and the Son are one
in the same and that of the same. The knowledge of the Father
needs to be translated to the Son. So that he can develop a clear
understanding of his own. He needs to be taught identity so that his
mind will function with free will. He absolutely needs to be
provided with the truth to purge him of the lies prevalent in today's
society. He needs to be taught about himself. He needs to learn to
constructively criticize and destructively compliment if necessary.
Then and only then after those lessons have sunk in can he become
a man ready for all the World will throw at him. Every Man and
Woman within a given community must adhere to the proper
development of the Children. There should be some sort of
accountability. Mentorship is an important part of the development
of young Men. I don't mean some Priest hanging with bunch of

young boys because it turns him on in some sick way. I mean everyday Men in all walks of life. This will not only help community relations because the young can start identifying with the old again. It will also give young men examples of men performing the duties of everyday life. Leadership by example also will show the younger generation that more exist in life than the fantasy lives portrayed on television. If we don't raise our children the television will. Right now lots of young people base the way they wanna life their lives on what they see on television. They also spend more time per week in front of the television than any other activity. It has become the baby sitter, the teacher, and for some basically a religion. Every thing they see on television they believe. So if some Rapper says its cool to hustle because you'll acquire diamonds, furs, flashy cars, all the money you can spend, and any woman of your desire. This is believed by the child because it comes from his or her greatest influence. There was no mention of the consequences of the actions. The children can follow the ill advice of his or her hero and find themselves in a world of trouble. So turn off the television at least once a week. I don't care what show is coming on. Your children are certainly worth it. Make up family activities, or discuss current events that affect you all. Put in the time now before it's too late. This will pay off ten fold in their future. All the babies will become the future thinkers who will maybe have to take care of you in your old age. Who would you rather have as their major influence you, or someone who might be motivated by something other than the development of our babies to build a bright future? I can't stress enough how important teaching the babies will be. After all it is thru them that our legacy goes on. This is how we live forever through the proper development of our children.

Chapter 9

Spin Doctors

If a news anchor says "Terror Threat", or "Weapons of Mass Destruction", many people shudder and go thru some form of mental preparedness for the worst. This is the trick being used to take away the rights of the hypnotized individuals to keep them in constant fear. Fear is a great tool used by the individuals in power. As long as they attach the key phrases they can erase law in the name of protecting you. There are people whose whole career is based on telling lies or twisting the truth into a form that suits Government goals. Think about the fact that after perhaps the greatest tragedy in the history of The United States. There was no investigation 911 was blamed on Osama Bin Laden after three days. There was no world wide investigation conducted. He even denied responsibility in the beginning. Saying that he had nothing to do with it but wished he had. As bad as this may seem don't Terrorist always claim responsibility for their actions because it is to further their cause. Why do you think no American newspapers reported the Insider Scandal that other major papers in the World all reported as at least suspicious? I mean if I put 15 Billion Dollars worth of fire insurance on my house and the next week it burnt to the ground by any purposeful act I'm sure the investigation would be long, deep and wide. Especially if I went on vacation along with all my friends, and family who lived there the day before and took all my valuables. What is the result of that investigation? Why isn't that as big an issue as the crap that was crammed down our throats about Weapons of Mass Destruction? Here we have a failing President who stuck up the whole country the previous January with his brother's Electoral Vote high jinks. Who had been completely absent as a leader in the wake of the uncovered charade. Now has the opportunity to cast himself in a new light and make billions in the process. "First we will steal the opium so the CIA can continue to distribute. Only now it is free so there is no investment it is all profit. Then we will move on to the Oil. Which is more my cup of tea being an Oil Man by trade myself". Even now as the stolen Oil flows onto tankers out of Iraq. We the Americans pay double at the pump. Our President profits directly on both ends of this. Why isn't that on the news every night? Instead of Anna Nicole Smith for two months. (No disrespect intended. Peace and Blessings be upon the family of the late Anna Nicole Smith. My condolences, and May she rest in peace.) The point is we are getting the short end of the stick on one hand and the long end of something else up the keister. Are you beginning to see a pattern? Are your eyes opening yet? This Administration can get away with anything it seems and all they have to do it say "Terror Threat from model airplanes", and everybody forgets the real issues. Knowledge is infinite so we shouldn't accept the few facts and figures presented to us on face value. Everything should be investigated when it comes to this administration. They feel they can do anything without consequence. The Vice President shot his man in the face while Quail Hunting. Have you ever seen Quail Hunting? The men line up in a line and the Quail are stirred up in front of them. So how do you shoot the man next to you? By Mistake?!? Come on. The Military Personnel have been instructed to do whatever is necessary to strike fear into The Iraqi People. They have been further told they will not be held at consequence. Who makes these kinds of General Orders? Is that not Terrorism? Is that not what we claim to be fighting against? Who is to be held responsible for these incorrigible acts? Is this not Genocide wasting the lives of thousands of American Soldiers and millions of Iraqis for profit. Extermination of a people on that scale reminds me of the Hitler Regime. Wait a min The Bushes were involved in that one too. Is it jumping out at you yet? Now think about who controls the media and what you are led to believe. Are all these things a coincidence or a great devilish plan? The time has come to look through the fear, along with all the other smoke and mirrors presented to us by Good Government. Wake up and smell the coffee or wake up with burns on your chest. The time for action is now, any action whatever you decide. But DAMMIT DO SOMETHING before it's too late for us all.

Chapter 10

To the projects

So in the long journey form the Western Shores of Africa here my
people stand. Most unable to identify with anything as far as
culture, or country. Many unable to identify with themselves. Is
there a grand design behind why these people hate each other and
themselves so much? I say there is. Everything that is bad in the
entire World is associated with Black. You know Black: hearted,
out(to), Death(the), Plague, hole, Ops, cat(bad luck), Sabbath,
Monday, sleep, magic, arts, sheep, ball(to), hand(the), cloud,
widow, helicopters, and Men (in). So how do we build our self
esteem? How do we identify with Africa when everything about
that is bad too; Africanized bees, West Nile Virus, Ebola,
Starvation, filth, disease, poverty, and Jungle People. So if we
don't have any reason to love ourselves, or any country to identify
with. We will be doomed to wander aimlessly through life and the
only hope will be that we don't fall victim to the streets, the
military, the police, obtain crippling injuries, or go to the cemetery
early. We should then only look forward to being an automaton of
some sort in some dead end job and being happy about it, because
we have cable, designer clothes and shoes, beer, weed, cocaine,
heroine or some sexual desire is being fulfilled all the while we
draw closer back to physical bondage. Why do think the new
schools that come up in our communities have no windows? Could
they double as internment centers? Is it that our children don't
need any sunlight? Do you think our children are subconsciously
being prepared for incarceration? Why do you think the Projects
were built to help the poor disenfranchised people? Hell No to
practice stacking a thousand families on top of each other in the
confines of one city block. If you have a community where there
are 3000 families all living on one city block there probably isn't
any community center that can handle all those children. There too
many people so resources dry up fast. What's left? The children

play in the street and eventually get turned on to Street Life in some fashion or form. The vicious cycle begins anew. We need to know and understand very few of these things happen by accident. I'm willing to say because this will probably be my last chance to tell you. Our president is a devil worshipper, whose oath to The United States meant little more to him than farting in the wind. His family has ties astronomical amounts of ill gotten monies for everything from the Land Grabbing Campaigns of the North after the Civil War, to Funding arming and supporting Hitler, to the farce of programs like Planned Parenthood The Peace Corps and USAID, To the development of AIDS in by mistake in the late seventies during Chemical Weapons Research (Project NAOMI), to in my opinion the shooting of Ronald W. Reagan, To the announcement of The New World Order September 12, 1991,to Rudolph Giuliani having advanced knowledge of the collapse of the World Trade Center Towers and warned no one (he admitted this in an interview with Peter Jennings on 9/11/01 and later recanted this), To the funding and supporting of Osama Bin Laden (hmm where have we seen that before???), to in my opinion blowing up the World Trade Center buildings for profit, to Giuliani clearing out rescue workers looking for survivors when they came across a cache of gold (proving it was more important to collect the gold during the tragedy than look for survivors)by the way the remains of many of those victims were never properly collect and about 40% of them went into trash receptacles, and to incite a war also SO PEOPLE WOULD FORGET HE'S NOT SUPPOSED TO BE OUR PRESIDENT ANY DAMN WAY, HE STOLE THE ELECTION WHO REMEMBERS THAT FAR BACK? Something like that should count as automatic disqualification from Government Service forever. The atrocities that have taken place in Afghanistan and Iraq should be called what they are War Crimes. If we all stand up we can change all of this. If not Ill probably go to prison for some crime I did not commit, or have an unfortunate accident sooner than later. I am prepared to accept my fate if my writings can touch just one person and set them on the path to change I have done my duty. This is an effort to cut the grass low the snakes have been exposing themselves for years. Now we must take a few heads to survive the times to come in peaceful harmony. Peace through realization and eventual understanding is my blessing to all.

Resources:

The Franklin Cover Up - John De Camp

George Bush : The Unauthorized Biography - Tarpley & Chaitkin

I Paid Hitler - Fritz Thyssen

School Restructuring – Pauline Lipman

Stumbling Toward Sustainability – John C. Denbach

Behold a Pale Horse – William Cooper

Google Video – Jessie Macbeth (Iraqi Veterans Against War)

CIA: An Instrument of Government – Arthur Burr Darling

Secret Warrior – Rodriguez & Weisman

America's Secret Establishment – Anthony C. Sutton

How The Order Creates War & Revolution – Anthony C. Sutton

History Of The Supreme Council – James David Carter

Breaking Points – Jack & Joanne Hinckley

The Politics Of The Rich And The Poor - Kevin Phillips

Stop Bush Rush To World War III – New Federalist Feb. 11, 1991

Portrait Of An Election – Elizabeth Drew

George W. Bush Speeches September 2001

The Men Behind Hitler
A German Warning To The World – Bernard Schreiber

AIDS And The Doctors Of Death – Allen Cantwell

Stolen Legacy – George G. M. James

They Came Before Columbus – Ivan Van Sertima

The Education Digest – John Henrik Clark

Ready For Revolution – Kwame Ture

United States Constitution And Amendments

Patriot Act I & Proposals For Patriot Act II

www.zietgiestthemovie.com

www.ingramcontent.com/pod-product-compliance
Lightning Source LLC
Chambersburg PA
CBHW061230280526
45784CB00006B/2708